FINGERPRINT DEVOTIONS

"*Fingerprint Devotions* is such a powerful and engaging devotional for kids ages eight to twelve. It's also a much needed one. We live in a society where children are bombarded daily with advertisements and social media posts that portray success as external beauty, money, and popularity, often making them feel like they don't 'measure up.' But in this devotional, kids will discover that they were uniquely created by Almighty God—from the hairs on their heads to their individual fingerprints. And readers will learn that God has an amazing plan and purpose for them. I can't wait to read this devotional with my grandkids!"

Michelle Medlock Adams
Multi-award-winning author
Including *Our God is Bigger Than That!* and *Dinosaur Devotions*

"Fun and fascinating! Tapping into the incredible uniqueness of fingerprints, Sandra Kay Chambers' *Fingerprint Devotions* invites children to explore the wonders of God all around and inside them, and like fingerprints—to leave a little of that wonder behind wherever they go!"

Tama Fortner
Award-winning author of more than fifty books
and the writer behind the million-selling *Indescribable Kids* series

"In *Fingerprint Devotions*, Sandra Kay Chambers beautifully weaves the child through discovering the unique imprint of God in their lives. In my clinical practice, I see common struggles among ages eight to twelve, such as loneliness, isolation, feeling misunderstood, poor self-image, and self-doubt. *Fingerprint Devotions* speak to all of those concerns, while guiding them to a closer relationship with God. Each devotional is short enough to draw the child in and then deepens their experience of God's presence through the fingerprint facts and guided prayer. What makes this devotional more impactful is the child is encouraged to value their purpose, continue to pursue God, and then make Him known to others. This is definitely a devotional that I will recommend in my clinical practice for children and families!"

Lori A. Cochard, MSW, LCSW
Licensed Clinical Social Worker

"This contemporary, interactive book of devotions for children will help them apply biblical truths to their everyday lives as they explore God's Word and His creation. Prayers, Bible verses, journal prompts, interesting fingerprint facts, and age-appropriate lessons combine to make an enjoyable and meaningful reading experience for kids. *Fingerprint Devotions* is sure to be a favorite with Christian families who want to grow in their faith journey."

Crystal Bowman
Bestselling, award-winning author of more than one hundred books for children and families
Author of *Our Daily Bread for Kids—365 Meaningful Moments with God.*

"If you're looking for an inspiring devotional for your eight-to-twelve-year-old child, I highly recommend *Fingerprint Devotions*. Sandra's conversational writing style is very enjoyable, and her fingerprint facts are fascinating to read. Her journaling ideas help your child think through what they've learned, and each devotional ends with a prayer to draw them closer to the Lord."

Kris Cox
Homeschool consultant, speaker, blogger and writer
Author of *Growing the Fruit of the Spirit*

"One of the keys to raising strong, confident children is teaching them that the God of the universe has made them uniquely on purpose for a purpose. As parents read *Fingerprint Devotions* and share in the learning of fingerprint facts while learning new scriptures with their children, they will be setting this very foundation to establish the God-confidence children need today to walk uprightly and justly. My identical twins and I loved this devotional book. While sharing these devotions with them, one of my girls said, 'I knew our fingerprints were different, but I didn't realize how truly unique God created each of us. Now I know we each have a different job we will do for God.'"

Staci B. Morgan, RN, MSN, PNP
Indiana Association of Home Educators—Special Learners Team Lead
Author and mother of four children, including identical twins

"In *Fingerprint Devotions*, a forty-day kid's devotional, your child will learn some inspiring facts about nature and the God revealed in His creation. As a pastor, I have worked with all ages of children during my pastoral ministry and with my own family of three boys and would love to have had this resource available. This devotional explores some of the wonders of creation as it reveals the uniqueness of each child. Kids will enjoy learning about the amazing qualities of our unique fingerprints and how this discovery helps connect us to the character and purpose of God. Children learn to appreciate the creativity and attention to detail of our caring, loving Heavenly Father. This devotional will help the young disciple draw closer to Jesus."

The Rev. Robin T. Adams
Retired Anglican pastor in the U.S., Ireland, and France

FINGERPRINT DEVOTIONS

40 DEVOTIONS TO HELP YOU REALIZE YOU ARE A KID UNIQUELY CREATED BY GOD FOR A PURPOSE

SANDRA KAY CHAMBERS

AMBASSADOR INTERNATIONAL
GREENVILLE, SOUTH CAROLINA & BELFAST, NORTHERN IRELAND

www.ambassador-international.com

FINGERPRINT DEVOTIONS
40 Devotions to Help You Realize You Are a Kid Uniquely Created by God for a Purpose

©2023 by Sandra Kay Chambers
All rights reserved

Hardcover ISBN: 978-1-64960-580-1
Paperback ISBN: 978-1-64960-542-9
eISBN: 978-1-64960-593-1

Cover Design by Hannah Linder Designs
Interior Typesetting by Dentelle Design
Edited by Bruce Stouffer

Ambassador International titles may be purchased in bulk for education, business, fundraising, or sales promotional use. For information, please email sales@emeraldhouse.com.

AMBASSADOR INTERNATIONAL
Emerald House
411 University Ridge, Suite B14
Greenville, SC 29601
United States
www.ambassador-international.com

AMBASSADOR BOOKS
The Mount
2 Woodstock Link
Belfast, BT6 8DD
Northern Ireland, United Kingdom
www.ambassadormedia.co.uk

The colophon is a trademark of Ambassador, a Christian publishing company.

Dedicated to a generation of kids who recognize they are created by God, endowed with gifts from Him, and called to make a difference in our world.

Contents

Introduction

Out of approximately 7.9 billion people on earth today, no two people have the same fingerprints. Each person's fingerprints are unique to them. God created you to be one of a kind, just like your fingerprints. There is no one else exactly like you, and He has a special purpose for your life. He created everything about you—the way you look, your strengths and weaknesses, your gifts and talents. You are one-of-a-kind in the entire universe, and He loves you just the way you are. He has also created you for a special purpose to be lived out right now and when you grow up.

In *Fingerprint Devotions*, you will explore some fun facts about fingerprints and learn that God's fingerprint has been on you even before you were born. Jesus also puts His fingerprint on you when you ask Him to come into your heart. Then, the Holy Spirit helps you be God's fingerprint to the world. You do this by showing love, kindness, and joy and by serving others through the unique gifts and talents He has given to you. You will also read about other young people just like you who used their gifts and talents to help others. Their efforts grew into nonprofits and organizations that helped many people in this country and around the world.

Each day there will be:

- a Scripture passage to read
- a devotion
- a fun fact about fingerprints or people who show God's fingerprint to the world
- a journal question or activity
- a prayer

Section I

God's Fingerprint Is On You By Creation

Day 1

God Created You In His Image

So God created mankind in his own image, in the image of God he created them; male and female he created them.

Genesis 1:27

In the beginning, God created a lot of things—stars and planets, animals and plants, the oceans and mountains—but only men and women were created in the image of God. That means you are very special to God because you were made to be like Him in many ways. God is creative, so you are creative, too. God loves people, so He created you to love people. God is the Master of science, and He gives people the ability to learn things about Him and His universe through science—and that includes you.

Not only are you special because you are created in His likeness, but you are also special because you are unique. Unique means "being the only one" or "being without a like or equal."[1] There is only one *YOU* in the entire universe! You may have the same color eyes or hair as someone else or even sort of look like them, but there is no one else exactly like you. You have a special purpose on earth that no one else has.

One of the amazing facts that proves you are unique are your fingerprints. God created you with your very own set of fingerprints that no one else has.

Fingerprint Fact

No two people have the same fingerprints, not even twins. And no single person has ever been found to have the same fingerprint on all fingers.[2]

Journal

Do you think of yourself as unique and special to God? In your journal, write down some ways you are different from your brother, sister, or friends (not just how you look, but also your likes and dislikes, what you are good at, your hobbies, etc.). Decorate your journal page with stickers, drawings, or pictures made using your own fingerprint. (See Resource Section in the back of this devotional to find out how to make these.)

Prayer

God, help me understand how special and unique I am to you. Help me believe You created me to be one of a kind to show Your love to others. Help me find my unique purpose now and when I grow up.

Day 2

God's Glory Is On Display

The heavens declare the glory of God; the skies proclaim the work of his hands. Day after day they pour forth speech; night after night they reveal knowledge. They have no speech, they use no words; no sound is heard from them. Yet their voice goes out into all the earth, their words to the ends of the world.

Psalms 19:1-4

The fingerprints of God are all around us! God's hand can be seen in the amazing design, pattern, and order of the universe, from its smallest atom to its billions of galaxies. Have you ever gone outside on a very dark night and looked up at the stars? Could you count them? Of course not—there are way too many. Scientists believe there are about one hundred to four hundred billion stars in the Milky Way Galaxy alone. Outside our galaxy are millions and millions of other galaxies. God's creation is so amazing, we cannot even imagine how big it is. Today's Scripture verse says that anyone who looks up at the heavens should be able to figure out how great God is because they can see His awesome creations—the sun, moon, stars, and planets.

God created all this, and yet He says He knows you personally and that you are special to Him. Never forget that no matter how small or how unimportant you may sometimes feel, God created you and has a special purpose for your life.

Fingerprint Fact

Leonardo Pisano, an Italian mathematician who lived from 1170 to 1250, discovered a design in all creation called the Fibonacci (Fee-bun-aw-chee) sequence. This important pattern shows up everywhere in nature. As a geometric form or picture, it is the shape of a spiral shell pattern. It is found in plants, animals, the center of our galaxy, and even our individual fingerprints.[3]

Journal

When you think about creation, what are you most amazed by—the stars and galaxies? The oceans and sea creatures? The forests and wild animals? Write down your answer in your journal and then look up more information online about God's creation or find a book on it the next time you go to the library.

Prayer

Lord, I thank You for all of creation. It is all amazing, but I especially thank You for _____. I want to learn more about this part of Your creation.

_____

_____

_____

_____

_____

_____

_____

_____

_____

_____

_____

_____

_____

_____

_____

_____

_____

_____

_____

_____

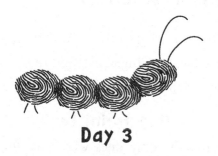

Day 3

Even the Animals Know Their Creator

"But ask the animals, and they will teach you, or the birds in the sky, and they will tell you; or speak to the earth, and it will teach you, or let the fish in the sea inform you. Which of these does not know that the hand of the LORD has done this? In his hand is the life of every creature and the breath of all mankind."

Job 12:7-10

Even the animals know that it was God Who created them. Animals are smarter in this area than people who do not recognize God as their Creator. You may hear different ideas in school of how the universe came into being without God, but God says the people saying these things are foolish. A person can become so proud that he thinks he is smarter than God. But the wise man understands from the Bible that God created everything.

As you learn more about science and God, you need to ask God to show you His truth. Sometimes, what the world says about

21

science disagrees with what God says. You can discover the truth by reading the Bible, learning about God in church and Sunday school, and reading about Christian scientists.

Fingerprint Fact

People are not the only ones who have fingerprints. Apes, monkeys, chimpanzees, and koala bears all have fingerprints. The koala bear is one of the few mammals, other than primates, that has fingerprints. Even with an electronic microscope, it can be quite difficult to distinguish between human and koala fingerprints.[4]

Journal

Do you remember in which order God created everything? If not, check out Genesis 1-2. Make a chart or draw a picture for each day of creation.

Prayer

Lord, I believe You are the Creator of everything and that Your creation is awesome. I also believe You created me in Your image; so teach me what that means, so I can please You.

_____

_____

_____

_____

_____

_____

_____

_____

_____

_____

_____

_____

_____

_____

_____

_____

_____

_____

_____

_____

_____

_____

_____

Day 4

God Calls You By Name

"I have summoned you by name; you are mine."
Isaiah 43:1b

Have you ever wondered how God can remember your name when there are over seven billion people on earth today? The Bible says God named each and every star, and there are a lot more stars than there are people. "He determines the number of the stars and calls them each by name" (Psalm 147:4). So, remembering your name is not a big deal for God.

In the Bible, names were very important and often described some character trait of the person. God even changed people's names in the Bible to reflect a change in their character or their calling. Check out a few examples: Abram to Abraham (Gen. 17:5), Sarai to Sarah (Gen. 17:15), and Simon to Peter (Mark 3:16). God says that He will give you a new name in heaven: "I will also give that person a white stone with a new name written on it, known only to the one who receives it" (Rev. 2:17c).

Names are important because they are personal. If a friend says, "Hey you," when they want your attention, it does not feel very personal, does it? But when a friend or teacher calls you by your name, you feel special. You feel they know you and care about you. Your parents gave you your name when you were born, but God says He also "summons" (calls) you by name. That means you are very important to Him.

Fingerprint Fact

Although scientists and astronomers disagree on the exact number of galaxies and stars, they estimate there are about one hundred thousand million stars in the Milky Way alone. Outside that, there are millions upon millions of other galaxies also! But we do know that each star is unique with unique properties. No two stars are alike.[5] That means God has a pretty big database of star names to remember. So, your name is easy for Him to remember!

Journal

Write your name in your journal. Color or decorate it. Ask your parents why they named you what they did. Was it to honor a relative or friend or perhaps because they liked the meaning of your name? Look up the meaning of your name online or in a name book like *The Complete Christian Baby Name Book* by Nicole M. McGinnis or *The Name Book* by Dorothy Astoria.

Prayer

God, You said You have called me by name and that no matter what my parents named me or what my name means, I belong to you. Help me remember that You know me by name and that You care about me.

_____

_____

_____

_____

_____

_____

_____

_____

_____

_____

_____

_____

_____

_____

_____

_____

_____

_____

_____

Day 5

God Knows Every Detail About You

And we know that in all things God works for the good of those who love him, who have been called according to his purpose.

Romans 8:28

Have you ever been assigned to write a story in school about your summer vacation? It would not be a very interesting story if you just said, "I went to the beach. I ate ice cream. I played games with my family." Details and descriptions are what help make your story interesting. "I went to the beach everyday and played in the waves and built sandcastles on the beach. I had a chocolate ice cream bar almost every day from the ice cream cart that came up and down the beach. I played a lot of my favorite board games in the evenings with my family." The details bring your story to life and make it fun to read.

God knows all the details of your life. He knows your likes and dislikes. He knows all your circumstances—the good things that have happened to you and the bad things. He knows when you struggle at home or at school. He knows everything is not perfect in your life. But He promises He will always be with you and that you can trust Him to work out all the details for your good. Although you may not see how right now, God will use everything in your life to bring you closer to Him.

Fingerprint Fact

Fingerprints have three basic patterns—loops, whorls, and arches. But the small details of your fingerprint, called "minutiae," are what analysts use to identify your specific fingerprints.[6]

Journal

Write down the things you like about yourself and the things you do not like about yourself. Write down some of the things you do well—art, music, sports, etc. Write down some of the things you wish you did well.

Prayer

God, help me to trust You with my life. Help me to believe that You work all things together—the good and even the bad—and have a special purpose for my life.

_____

_____

_____

_____

_____

_____

_____

_____

_____

_____

_____

_____

_____

_____

_____

_____

_____

_____

_____

_____

_____

_____

_____

Day 6

God Knows How Many Hairs You Have

And even the very hairs of your head are all numbered.
Matthew 10:30

When you brush your hair, do you notice that some strands of hair show up in your hairbrush or in the sink? Girls probably notice this more than guys, especially if they have long hair. According to the American Academy of Dermatologists, it is normal to lose anywhere from fifty to one hundred strands of hair each day; but since there are one hundred thousand or more hair follicles on each person's scalp, the loss of one hundred or so hair strands a day does not make a big difference in appearance.

The Bible says God knows exactly how many hairs you have on your head; and since you lose some every day, that means He is watching over you every single day! Not only does He know how many hairs are on your head each day, but He also knows all the things you are going through. He knows when you hurt outside or inside. He knows when you succeed at something or fail at something. He knows your dreams and your fears, and He promises to never leave you. You can trust God.

Fingerprint Fact

Even your hair has a unique fingerprint. As many as one thousand protein markers can be used to identify individuals and distinguish one person from another.[7]

Journal

Do you believe God cares for you that much? What makes you doubt God's care? Make a list in your journal of all the times in the past that God has taken care of you. When you have times that you doubt that God is there or is looking out for you, reread this list to remind yourself of God's faithfulness.

Prayer

God, thank You for caring for me so much that You even keep track of the hairs on my head. Help me to always remember and thank You for caring for me.

_____

_____

_____

_____

_____

_____

_____

_____

_____

_____

_____

_____

_____

_____

_____

_____

_____

_____

_____

_____

_____

_____

_____

_____

Day 7

You Are God's Handiwork

For we are God's handiwork, created in Christ Jesus to do good works, which God prepared in advance for us to do.
Ephesians 2:10

Handiwork is something that one has made or done by hand. You were created by God's own hand, so you are His handiwork. You are unique. You were not created by a machine on an assembly line like a car.

Have you ever seen your mom or grandmother working on a knitting or embroidery project? They use thread or yarn to create a beautiful pattern on material. On the right side, it is a beautiful creation or handiwork; but if you look at the back of it, it is just a mess of different threads. Sometimes, we feel that way about our lives, but God does not see the messy back side—He sees the beautiful finished product. As you grow and seek God, He will reveal more and more about Himself to you. He will also help you use the gifts and talents He has given you to honor Him and serve others. The Bible says He prepared good works for you to do because He wants you to be His fingerprint in the world, showing His goodness, love, and purpose.

Fingerprint Fact

Fingerprints are unique patterns made by friction ridges (mountains) and furrows (valleys) that appear on the pad of the fingers and thumb. Prints from palms, toes, and feet are also unique; however, they are used less often for identification.[8]

Journal

Do you sometimes feel like your life is a mess? Copy the Scripture above in your journal. Decorate your journal page and memorize the Scripture verse.

Prayer

God, help me believe I am Your beautiful handiwork and help me discover those good works You created me to do.

_____

_____

_____

_____

_____

_____

_____

_____

_____

_____

_____

_____

_____

_____

_____

_____

_____

_____

_____

_____

_____

_____

_____

_____

Day 8

God Thinks About You All The Time

How precious to me are your thoughts, God!
How vast is the sum of them!

Psalm 139:17

When you are excited about something like your birthday, Christmas, or an upcoming vacation trip, you cannot stop thinking about it. You are so excited that sometimes you cannot even sleep! God feels the same way about you. He is so excited, He cannot stop thinking about you.

God made plans for your life even before you were born, and He is excited to watch you grow and use the gifts He has given you. Since you are always in His thoughts, you can be sure He is always watching over you. You do not have to be afraid, and you are never alone. You can always talk to God about anything that is on your mind.

God also wants you to think about the things that please Him. The Bible says we are to think about those things that are true, pure, right, holy, friendly, and proper (Phil. 4:8). He wants us to be careful about what we let into our minds—what we watch on TV or on social media. He also wants us to think good thoughts about others and be kind to them.

Fingerprint Fact

Criminals have been trying to remove their fingerprints for years. However, it is almost impossible to do so permanently because the pattern of your fingerprints is more than skin-deep.[9] You can also be sure that you will never be removed from God's thoughts!

Journal

Are you surprised that God thinks about you all the time? Why or why not? How does knowing God cares about you that much make you feel? Draw a picture to show your feelings.

Prayer

God, thank You that You love me so much that You think about me all the time. Thank You that You are always there to take care of me.

_____
_____
_____
_____
_____
_____
_____
_____
_____
_____
_____
_____
_____
_____
_____
_____
_____
_____
_____
_____
_____
_____
_____
_____

Day 9

God Puts His Autograph On You

You did not choose me, but I chose you and appointed you so that you might go and bear fruit.

John 15:16

Have you ever gotten an autograph—maybe from a sports star or an author of one of your favorite books? You value that person's autograph because he or she is famous and means something to you. Famous painters also sign their own paintings to show they are the creators of their work. Authors autograph their books to show that they wrote them. Creators are proud of what they have created, and so is God.

When you were still in your mother's womb, God put his autograph on you. He said that you were His creation and that you were important to Him. You were chosen by Him, and He has a plan for your life. Your purpose right now is to learn more about God and yourself and to discover your special gifts and talents. You were also created so you could show God's fingerprint to those around you. You can be an example of God's love and kindness and of how God wants people to live while on earth.

Fingerprint Fact

The name for the study of fingerprints is *dermatoglyphics* (der-ma-to-glif-ics). It means "the science of the study of skin patterns" and was first used in 1926.[10]

Journal

Do you believe that God created you as one of a kind with a special purpose for your life? Why or why not? If you do believe that God created you and put His autograph on you, how does that make a difference in your life?

Prayer

God, thank You for creating me to be different from everyone else on earth, just like my fingerprints are different from everyone else's. Help me discover my unique gifts and talents and the purpose You have for me.

Day 10

You Are God's Masterpiece

For you created my inmost being; you knit me together
in my mother's womb. I praise you because I am fearfully
and wonderfully made; your works are wonderful, I
know that full well.

Psalm 139:13-14

Have you ever visited a museum to see a famous painting? There are many paintings that are considered masterpieces, such as the *Mona Lisa* by Leonardo da Vinci. What makes a painting a masterpiece? A masterpiece shows a special type of originality that captures the imagination.

Leonardo da Vinci used several new techniques to paint the *Mona Lisa*. His painting changed the rules of art at the time, and these methods became a part of what is now taught in art schools. Today, the *Mona Lisa* is valued at 867 million dollars.

You are worth far more to God than the *Mona Lisa* or any other earthly masterpiece. You are God's masterpiece—one of a kind! You are unique and original. No one else is like you. God has created you to do good things that show His fingerprint to the world.

Fingerprint Fact

After looking through paintings of Leonardo da Vinci for three years, forensic scientists found a single, complete fingerprint on one of his paintings. The print was of his left index finger on his painting *Portrait of a Lady with an Ermine,* painted around 1490.[11]

Journal

What kind of paintings do you like? Pictures with lots of color? Pictures of beautiful mountains or lakes? Pictures of people or animals? Do you like to draw, paint, or create things? Because God is creative, He has made you creative, so you can reflect who He is. Decorate your journal today in some creative way.

Prayer

Lord, help me to see myself as a masterpiece created by You.

Section 2

God's Fingerprint Is On You Through Jesus

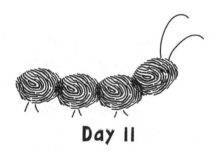

Day 11

Jesus Wants To Live In Your Heart

For God so loved the world that he gave his one and only Son, that whoever believes in him shall not perish but have eternal life.

John 3:16

Is it not amazing that the most creative, loving, and powerful Being in the universe wants to live in your heart to encourage you, guide you, and give you peace and joy? When God created Adam and Eve, His plan was for them to know Him like this; but Adam and Eve disobeyed God. Disobedience to God is called sin, and sin separates us from God. When Adam and Eve sinned, it created a wall between them and God and also between God and all future generations.

But God loved people so much that He had a plan to save them. He sent Jesus to be born and grow up as a human being to show us what He is like and how we should live. He also sent Jesus to take the punishment for our sin by dying on the cross. Now, we can be with God in Heaven forever, but that is not all. Now, we can walk and talk with God every day because we are forgiven.

When you ask Jesus to come into your heart, you are asking Him to come and take charge of your life because your heart represents the total of who you are. You are saying to God, "I believe that Jesus came to earth to take the punishment for my sin. And I believe that You want me to know You and that You have a purpose for my life."

Fingerprint Fact

Our fingerprints never change over our lifetimes, just like God's love and care for us never changes.[12]

Journal

Have you ever asked Jesus to come into your life? If you have, write in your journal when you did this. If not, pray the prayer below and write down the date you did this in your journal. Then tell someone—your parents or a friend—that you asked Jesus into your heart today!

Prayer

Jesus, thank You for coming to Earth and dying to take away all my sin now and forever. I invite You into my heart and into my life to lead and guide me. Teach me and show me Your purpose for my life.

_____
_____
_____
_____
_____
_____
_____
_____
_____
_____
_____
_____
_____
_____
_____
_____
_____
_____
_____
_____
_____
_____

Day 12

You Are A New Person In Christ

Therefore, if anyone is in Christ, the new creation has come: The old has gone, the new is here.

2 Corinthians 5:17

Do you sometimes wish you were someone else? Do you wish you could erase some of the bad stuff in your life and start all over? Well, guess what—you can. When you ask Jesus into your heart, the Bible says you are "re-born." That means you are a brand-new person with a brand-new life ahead of you. You are born into God's kingdom, and you have a new heart. It is like you got a heart transplant, and you now have the ability to obey and follow God.

You also have the Holy Spirit living in you to help you obey God and please Him. That does not mean you will be perfect, but God will always be there to forgive you and help you please Him and become more like Him. God says He forgives your past sins and future sins—all you need to do when you sin is ask Him to forgive you and help you live for Him.

When you are born again, you shine in such a way that others will notice the change in you. You will be a light to others. It is the life of Jesus shining in and through you that sets you apart from the world and helps you be God's fingerprint to the world. You are called to show others how much God loves them and how much He wants them to become His children just like you did when you asked Jesus into your heart.

Fingerprint Fact

Fingerprints are thought to serve two purposes. First, they help us grip objects. Second, they increase the sensitivity of our touch and allow us to feel the textures and shapes of things.[13] Similarly, when you become a new person in Christ, you have a new purpose in life and become more sensitive to God's voice and to what pleases Him.

Journal

Write a letter to God in your journal thanking Him for Jesus, the One Who made it possible for you to become a brand-new person. Ask Him to help you live the life He has planned for you and to help you show His love to others.

Prayer

Lord, I am so glad You died so that I could be reborn, have a heart transplant, and become a new person. Help me to live the new life You have planned for me.

_____

_____

_____

_____

_____

_____

_____

_____

_____

_____

_____

_____

_____

_____

_____

_____

_____

_____

_____

_____

_____

_____

_____

Day 13

The Holy Spirit Guides You

And I will ask the Father, and he will give you another advocate to help you and be with you forever—the Spirit of truth.

John 14:16-17

After Jesus' death, His disciples missed Him and felt very sad. They felt like orphans. But before His death, Jesus told His disciples He would not leave them as orphans, but He would send them another Advocate (a person who supports another) to be with them after He returned to Heaven. Jesus said that this Advocate, the Holy Spirit, would remind them of His teachings, lead them into all truth, and be with them forever. Jesus also promised them His peace.

The Holy Spirit is not a scary ghost; He is God in you. He is the One Who helps you get to know God better and obey Him. He helps you understand what the Bible has to say about God and Jesus. The Holy Spirit will never say anything bad about Jesus or anything different from what the Bible says. He will never tell you to do anything that contradicts what the Bible says. The Holy Spirit will also give you God's peace. He is the One Who exhibits all the fruit of the Spirit that you will learn about in the next section of our devotional. As you grow and learn more about God, you will learn to hear the Spirit's voice and guidance better and better.

Fingerprint Fact

Your ears are unique in size, shape, and structure, just like your fingerprints are unique.[14] God has also given you spiritual ears to hear His voice when He speaks to you.

Journal

Have you ever heard the Holy Spirit tell you something? Think about a time when perhaps you did not know what to do and then got an idea or direction that was from God. Write about that time in your journal. Then list all the things you know about the Holy Spirit and how He helps you follow God.

Prayer

Lord, thank You for the gift of the Holy Spirit. Help me learn to listen and obey when He speaks to me.

_____

_____

_____

_____

_____

_____

_____

_____

_____

_____

_____

_____

_____

_____

_____

_____

_____

_____

_____

_____

_____

_____

_____

_____

Day 14

God Gives You A Purpose

When I consider your heavens, the work of your fingers,
the moon and the stars, which you have set in place, what
is mankind that you are mindful of them, human beings
that you care for them.

Psalm 8:3-4

We have already learned that God is the Master Creator. Everything He created was perfect. God did not just create everything, sling it into space, and say, "I'm done. I think I'll go take a nap." The Bible says that when God created Adam and Eve, He created a beautiful garden for them. I bet there were colorful flowers and singing birds in the garden. There were also fruit trees with delicious fruit to eat. There was sunshine during the day and the light of the moon and twinkling stars at night.

Not only did God create everything Adam and Eve needed, but He also gave them a purpose. He gave them work to do. He told them to take care of the garden. Adam also got to name all the animals. That must have been fun!

God also has a purpose for your life. Your first purpose is to love God and get to know Him. You will discover what gifts and talents God has given you to fulfill your purpose as you grow. It will take work on your part to develop those gifts God has given you. Sometimes, it will be fun; and sometimes, it will be hard. Think about the chores you have to do. Those chores are not always fun, but they are important jobs that need to be done. And they help you learn responsibility and faithfulness. The Bible says, "Whatever you do, work at it with all your heart, as working for the Lord" (Col. 3:23).

Fingerprint Fact

"Dactyloscopy" (dak-tuh-los-kuh-pee) is the study of fingerprint identification. Fingerprint identification has many different purposes. It is used to identify crime victims, as evidence for crimes, for background checks, for security clearance, for employment, and to control access to secure areas.[15]

Journal

What purpose do you think God has for you right now? It might be as simple as learning to obey your parents, study hard in school, or be a good friend to someone. Write down your thoughts in your journal.

Prayer

God, I thank You that you have a purpose for my life, including right now. Help me to listen to You, obey You, and learn to trust You.

_____
_____
_____
_____
_____
_____
_____
_____
_____
_____
_____
_____
_____
_____
_____
_____
_____
_____
_____
_____
_____
_____
_____
_____
_____

Day 15

You Are Creative Because God Is Creative

How many are your works, LORD!
In wisdom you made them all.

Psalm 104:24

Did you know that Walt Disney was once told that he lacked imagination? But he did not believe that lie and look at what he created! You are creative because you are made in God's image, and He is creative. All your skills and abilities are a reflection of your Creator. With the help of the Holy Spirit living in you, you can be God's fingerprint through the creative gifts He has given you.

In the Old Testament, God gave skills to certain people for His purposes. When God wanted His tabernacle built, Moses said of the builders that "[God] has filled them with skill to do all kinds of work as engravers, designers, embroiderers in blue, purple and scarlet yarn and fine linen, and weavers—all of them skilled workers and designers" (Exod. 35:35).

There are lots of ways to show God's creativity in today's world. People who paint, write books, sing, or play an instrument reflect God's creativity. But architects, scientists, teachers, doctors, business leaders, pastors, and others also reflect God's creativity. He gives a wide variety of gifts to His children so they can show His creativity in the world.

Fingerprint Fact

There are three types of fingerprints:

1. Visible—those left by dirt, grease, blood, etc.
2. Impression—an indentation in soft material like butter, putty, tar, etc.
3. Latent—fingerprints that require processing to make visible and suitable for analysis.[16] God will use you to leave all kinds of fingerprints in the world to show His glory.

Journal

You will discover what gifts and talents you have as you grow. Write down some of the things you love to do right now. What are some things you would like to do when you grow up?

Prayer

God, I am creative because You are a creative God. You put certain desires in my heart, and You have given me certain gifts and talents. Help me to discover them as I grow and use them to help others and show Your love to those around me.

_____

_____

_____

_____

_____

_____

_____

_____

_____

_____

_____

_____

_____

_____

_____

_____

_____

_____

_____

_____

_____

_____

_____

_____

_____

Day 16

You Are A Member Of Christ's Body

Just as a body, though one, has many parts,
but all its many parts form one body, so it is with Christ.
I Corinthians 12:12

Have you ever cut your thumb on the hand you use the most? If so, you probably realized how important your thumb is, even though it is only a small part of your body. With a hurt thumb, it is hard to do a lot of things—fasten a button, tie your shoe, brush your teeth, or even hold a pen to write.

God says every single part of His Body (the church) is important. Every Christian—no matter his or her age, size, appearance, or gifts—is important to God and to the Church. Without doing your part, however small it may seem, the church cannot do what it is supposed to do.

The Church is more than just the place you might go on Sundays for a church service or Sunday school. God wants His

Church to reach outside its doors to help people wherever they are—perhaps at your school or in your neighborhood.

There are many ways to be God's Church to the world. Maybe you could pray for someone in your class at school who is sick, or help a neighbor with yard work, or bake cookies for someone who is alone. Those are all important jobs. Whatever part you do helps make everything work together like it should and enables God to show His love to the world.

Fingerprint Fact

Even snowflakes have a unique fingerprint. No two snowflakes are exactly alike.[17] It takes a whole lot of snowflakes working together to cover the ground so you can build a snowman, make a snow angel, or go sledding. In the same way, it takes every member of the Body of Christ working together to do God's work on earth.

Journal

Have you ever thought you were too young or unimportant to do anything for God? Think about your thumb the next time you see a job you could do. In your journal, make a list of some of the things you might do this week as a member of Christ's Body, the Church.

Prayer

God, help me realize that I am an important part of the
Body of Christ, no matter what my age is. Show me things
I can do as a member of Your Body to show Your love to
the world.

_____

_____

_____

_____

_____

_____

_____

_____

_____

_____

_____

_____

_____

_____

_____

_____

_____

_____

_____

_____

_____

_____

_____

Day 17

God Watches Over You As You Grow

**And Jesus grew in wisdom and stature,
and in favor with God and man.**

Luke 2:52

J esus was born into the world as a human baby, and He grew into a child and teen just like you. Jesus played as a child like you. He probably had chores, and He learned carpenter skills from His father. He also learned things about Himself and about God. He read God's Word, learned to pray, and learned to hear God speak to Him. God watches over you as you grow, just as He did His very own Son. God wants you to develop good character traits as you grow that will help you become the person God created you to be. Below are a few character traits you can begin to work on right now.

- Are you *teachable*? Do you listen to and learn from your parents, teachers, Sunday school teacher, pastor, and other adults in your life?

- Are you *responsible?* Do you do your chores without grumbling? Do you finish your homework? Do you always follow through when you promise to do something?

- Do you have *perseverance?* This means you do not give up easily. You keep trying, even when something is hard. Do you have a subject in school that is hard for you? Do you keep working at it? Do you keep practicing that musical instrument you wanted to play, even though some days you would rather be outside playing?

Fingerprint Fact

Fingerprints develop during the tenth week of pregnancy and are fully formed at six months.[18] God watched over you in your mother's womb and continues to watch over you all your life.

Journal

What character traits do you need to work on? Choose one of the above character traits to work on this week. Write down some ways you could work on it.

Prayer

Lord, help me to believe You are watching over me every day and that You have a purpose for me. I want to have good character traits, so help me this week with the one I have chosen to work on.

_____

_____

_____

_____

_____

_____

_____

_____

_____

_____

_____

_____

_____

_____

_____

_____

_____

_____

_____

_____

_____

_____

Day 18

God Wants To Be Your Friend

I no longer call you servants, because a servant does not know his master's business. Instead, I have called you friends, for everything that I learned from my Father I have made known to you.

John 15:15

Best friends are great because they like some of the same things you do. You enjoy talking with your best friend and maybe even sharing secrets. You both may be in the same class at school or play sports together or belong to the same group or club.

When you invited Jesus into your heart, Jesus became your best Friend. You can talk to Him just like you talk to your other friends. You can tell Him anything, and He always listens. He promises to always be with you, guide you, and help you.

Your best friend may change as you grow. He or she may move to a new school or to a new state. You both may develop new interests and hobbies and find new best friends. However, Jesus will never stop being your best Friend. He never leaves you.

Fingerprint Fact

Here's a fun fact about another best friend you might have— your dog! Just as humans can be identified by their fingerprints, dogs can be identified by their noseprints. A dog's noseprint is unique, just as human fingerprints are unique. A few places in the United States have already adopted dog noseprinting as a way of identifying lost dogs. The Canadian Kennel Club has been accepting dog noseprints as proof of identity since 1938.[19]

Journal

Write the name of your best friend in your journal. Why is he or she your best friend? What qualities make him or her a good best friend? If you do not have a best friend yet, ask God to give you one.

Prayer

God, help me remember that You want to be my best Friend. You want me to talk with You just like I talk to my friends. I can trust You to listen to anything I need to talk about.

_____

_____

_____

_____

_____

_____

_____

_____

_____

_____

_____

_____

_____

_____

_____

_____

_____

_____

_____

_____

_____

_____

_____

_____

_____

_____

_____

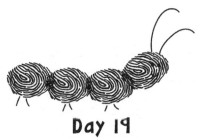

Day 19

Learn To Trust God

Trust in the LORD with all your heart and lean not on your own understanding; in all your ways submit to him, and he will make your paths straight.

Proverbs 3:5-6

Do you ever wish you were someone else or that you lived somewhere else? Do you wish that you were prettier or stronger? God created you inside and outside—your hair color, your eyes, how tall you are. He created you with likes and dislikes. He gave you certain strengths, and He knows your every weakness.

Right now, you are growing and learning about yourself. Some things you like about yourself, and some things you wish were different. A year from now, you will think differently about a lot of things. Five years from now, you will look different and will have discovered gifts and talents you never knew you had. You will add new friends, and your outlook on life will change. Never get stuck where you are. Never get discouraged or depressed. Change comes with every season of your life. Never lose hope because God promises He will work all things together for your good if you trust Him. He will use all things—the good and the bad—to make you into the person He wants you to be.

Fingerprint Fact

Zebras and tigers have the equivalent of fingerprints on their fur markings. The patterns that form the lines and spots are unique for each individual animal.[20] Animals do not try to change the way they look because they know God created them perfectly.

Journal

Have you ever felt stuck—like things will never change in your life? Maybe you are discouraged or depressed (really, really sad)? Just remember that things won't stay the same forever. And God has promised that He will work all things together for your good. Write down a time you didn't like something about yourself or felt discouraged, and then things changed for the better. Thank God for helping you through this time. If you are in one of those times right now, pray the prayer below and trust God to bring you through it.

Prayer

God, help me to trust You with my life. Help me to believe that You work all things together—the good and bad— and that You have a special purpose for my life.

_____

_____

_____

_____

_____

_____

_____

_____

_____

_____

_____

_____

_____

_____

_____

_____

_____

_____

_____

_____

_____

_____

_____

Day 20

Talk To God In Prayer

Do not be anxious about anything, but in every situation, by prayer and petition, with thanksgiving, present your requests to God.

Philippians 4:6

Have you ever created a secret code or language so that you and your friends could communicate with each other? Only those who were invited into the group could know and use that secret code. Prayer is sort of like a secret code that God gives to His children so they can communicate with Him. He says you can use prayer to talk to Him anytime about anything.

In the Lord's Prayer that Jesus taught His disciples, He says you can ask God for the things you need every day—food, clothing, protection, guidance, etc. God also wants you to pray for other people and their needs. You can pray for others to know Him and for God to meet their needs. You can also pray for your church and pray that leaders in our nation would obey and please God. You can pray for missionaries and for the people around the world they are trying to reach with the Gospel. You can be God's prayer warrior to help bring about His will on earth.

There are many different types of prayers. Thanksgiving is a form of prayer, and it is good to thank God every day for all the gifts He gives to you. Some other prayers, like the Lord's Prayer, you may pray in church. There are prayers people pray before meals to thank God for their food. There are bedtime prayers you may pray with your parents. But prayer can also just be talking to God as a Friend. You can do this anytime and anywhere. He is always there to listen.

Fingerprint Fact

Fingerprints have been established as the "barcode" that identifies each individual in the human species.[21] Just as our fingerprints are like a unique barcode, so our relationship with God in prayer is unique. We do not have to pray any certain way for God to hear us.

Journal

Write down a prayer of thanksgiving to God, a prayer for something you need, and a prayer for someone else.

Pray

Lord, thank You that You want to hear from me and that I can pray about anything for myself, my family, and others.

_____
_____
_____
_____
_____
_____
_____
_____
_____
_____
_____
_____
_____
_____
_____
_____
_____
_____
_____
_____
_____
_____

Section 3

God's Fingerprint Is Shown By How You Live

Day 21

You Show The Fruit Of The Holy Spirit In Your Life

But the fruit of the Spirit is love, joy, forbearance, kindness, goodness, faithfulness, gentleness, and self-control. Against such things there is no law.
Galatians 5:22–23

Fruit is amazing. It comes in different colors and yummy flavors. It is something that looks and tastes good and is healthy for us. The Bible pictures the character traits God wants us to exhibit in our lives as the "fruit of the Spirit." Learning to show all this good fruit in our lives takes time because we do not automatically do everything perfectly when we become Christians. God is patient and gives us time to learn. We can ask the Holy Spirit to help us show God's good fruit in our lives. We can never show too much love, joy, peace, patience, kindness, goodness, faithfulness, gentleness, and self-control. When we show these fruits in our lives, we are showing God's fingerprint to the world.

In this section of our devotional, we will look at each character trait separately and also look at a biblical character who exhibited that trait in their life.

Fingerprint Fact

Our fingers have tiny sweat pores that leave fingerprints behind on whatever we touch.[22] Our lives also leave fingerprints, for good or bad. We need the Holy Spirit in our lives to help us leave good fingerprints.

Journal

What is your favorite fruit? What fruit of God's Spirit do you need God to grow in you? Write the name of that fruit in your journal.

Prayer

God, grow Your fruit in me, so I can be Your ngerprint to the world and show others Who You are and how much You love them.

Day 22

Love With God's Love

Do everything in love.

1 Corinthians 16:14

The Bible tells us God is Love—everything He does is done from love. He is also the source of love. He loved us first; and because we have His love inside of us, we can love others. So, how do we love others? First, we look to see what *they* need instead of always thinking of what we need or want. That is hard sometimes because we are naturally selfish and want things for ourselves. But when God's love is in us, we love others first. Instead of always wanting our way, we let our brother, sister, or friends have their way.

If we have God's love in us, we also think good thoughts about others. We think of them as being as important as we are. We do not call people names or bully them. We stand up for others, and we show them that we care about them. We may not always feel like loving people, especially those who hurt us or who are unkind, but we need to ask God to help us love them.

In the Bible, Ruth showed love to her mother-in-law, Naomi, by not deserting her when she wanted to return to her home country of Israel. Ruth went with her and committed to follow her God. God rewarded Ruth for her love and loyalty and provided a husband for Ruth who would care for them both. Ruth became part of the line of Jesus Christ Himself (Ruth 1:16).

Fingerprint Fact

A very rare genetic condition can prevent fingerprints from forming at all.[23] Sin in our life can also prevent us from loving others and showing God's fingerprint of love. But all we need to do is confess our sin and ask God to help us show His love.

Journal

Is there someone you have a hard time loving? What is a way you could show God's love to them?

Prayer

Lord, I do not feel like loving _____, but please help me to love them with Your love. Help me nd a way to show love to them.

Day 23

Be Filled With God's Joy

May the God of hope fill you with all joy and peace as you
trust in him, so that you may overflow with hope by the
power of the Holy Spirit.

Romans 15:13

Happiness is the feeling you get when you get a gift or when
Dad or Mom hug you and tell you how proud they are of you.
We all like to be happy. God likes us to be happy, too, but there are
times when we do not feel happy. During those times, God says
we can still have joy because joy is not about what we have or how
we feel. It is not about our circumstances. Joy is about knowing
God is in charge and that He loves us whether we feel happy or
not. We can be joyful that God always loves us and that He will
never leave us. Sometimes, just singing a song, reading our Bibles,
and praying can help us feel joy again.

David is a good example of someone with God's joy in the
Bible. David did not just rejoice in God when things were going
well; he also praised God during difficult times, and he had plenty

of those. David had to run and hide from Saul, who wanted to kill him; but he did not let his fear determine his level of joy. He trusted in God. David wrote many of the psalms; and they show his joy in God even during his troubles, fears, doubts, and failures.

Fingerprint Fact

Your teeth also have a unique fingerprint. Every tooth in your mouth is unique to you and completely different from those of any other person on earth. That means that every person's bite and smile are unique to them.[24] Your smile is one way you can easily show your joy to others.

Journal

Write down a few of the times when you felt happy. Then, write down times you experienced God's joy even when things were not going well and you did not feel happy.

Prayer

God, help me to always be joyful because You love me and because Jesus lives in my heart. Even when I do not feel happy, help me to be joyful and to be Your ngerprint of joy to the world.

_____

_____

_____

_____

_____

_____

_____

_____

_____

_____

_____

_____

_____

_____

_____

_____

_____

_____

_____

_____

Day 24

Live In Peace

**Now may the Lord of peace himself give you peace
at all times and in every way.**

2 Thessalonians 3:16

Have you ever worried about something—like someone not liking you or trying to cause a fight? It can cause you to be upset and feel bad inside. You may want to get angry and get back at that person, but God says He wants you to show His peace instead.

Peace comes when we trust God and believe He loves us and will never leave us, even in difficult times. His peace will help us act peacefully toward others and not get in arguments or fights. When we experience God's peace, we are not worrying or being anxious about what will happen. We are not trying to make things happen the way we think they should or the way we want them to. We are trusting that God will take care of things. We can rest in Him. We can have peaceful sleep and dreams.

The story of Joseph in the Bible shows a young man who had God's peace in his heart, even in hard times. His brothers hated him and sold him into slavery because God had given him a dream that he would rule over them. He was even thrown in prison, but Joseph trusted God. Eventually, Joseph was promoted to the second highest position in Egypt. God used Joseph to save his entire family and Egypt from a famine. Joseph forgave his brothers and never sought revenge because he recognized God's hand in everything that happened (Gen. 37-50).

Fingerprint Fact

Today, digital scanners are used to capture images of fingerprints. To create a digital fingerprint, a person places his or her finger on an optical or silicon reader surface and holds it there for a few seconds. The reader converts the information from the scan into digital data patterns. The computer then maps the points on the fingerprints and uses those points to search for similar patterns in the database.[25] God's database, the Bible, gives us a list of the fruit of the Spirit that He wants us to exhibit to the world.

Journal

Write down some ways you can know God's peace. Then write down some ways you can show peace to others.

Prayer

Lord, help me to trust You, so I do not get anxious or worried. Help me to remember to pray for Your peace in my heart so I can show others Your fingerprint of peace in my life.

Day 25

Practice Patience

For in this hope we were saved. But hope that is seen is no hope at all. Who hopes for what they already have? But if we hope for what we do not yet have, we wait for it patiently.

Romans 8:24-25

I t is hard to be patient when it is Christmas Eve or the day before your birthday. You are so excited to open your gifts that you can hardly wait. But that is not the only time you need patience. You need God's patience when you do not know what your future will be like. You may be having a hard time in school or in your family. You may have prayed and prayed for something, but God still has not answered.

During those hard times that you do not understand, you need God's patience. He may be wanting to teach you something that will help you be more like Him. Or He may be waiting to give you something even better than what you asked for. God is always good, and He always give you what is best. Trust Him while you wait in patience. If you do that, you will become more like Him and show others His fingerprint through your patience.

Noah showed great patience and trust in God when He told him to build an ark because it was going to rain and destroy all living things on earth. Some Bible scholars believe it took Noah forty days to build the ark. Others believe it took much longer—even years—to build. After it was built and Noah had gathered all the animals aboard, he still had to have patience and trust that God would bring the ark safely to dry land (Gen. 6:11-22).

Fingerprint Fact

Fingerprints are even more unique than DNA, the genetic material in each of our cells. Although identical twins can share the same DNA—or at least most of it—they cannot have the same fingerprints.[26] All of us need God's patience, but how each of us shows it will be different.

Journal

Was there a time this week when you showed God's patience? Write about it in your journal. Was there a time when you were impatient? Ask God to help you grow the fruit of patience in your life.

Prayer

God, help me learn to be patient when I am having a hard time. Help me to trust You and wait for Your answer.

Day 26

Show God's Goodness

"No one is good—except God alone."

Mark 10:18

T he Bible says no one is good except for God. But when Jesus comes into your heart, He helps you be good. Goodness means you always do the right thing, even if others do not. It means you are not afraid to stand up for what is right. You do not care if others laugh at you or mock you for not doing what they are doing. You care more about what God thinks of you than what others think.

Goodness is also helping others. Jesus always put others first. He healed those who were sick, and He died for everyone so that they could be forgiven and have a new life with Him both now and forever.

In the Bible, Tabitha (also called Dorcas) showed God's goodness to others. She was always doing good and helping the poor and making clothes for those in need. When Tabitha became sick and died, Peter prayed for her, and she came back to life (Acts 9:36-43).

Fingerprint Fact

Neolithic bricks from the ancient city of Jericho were discovered to contain thumbprints of the bricklayers.[27] We leave behind God's fingerprint of goodness when we do good deeds for others.

Journal

Have you ever stood up for what is right, even when others made fun of you? Write down a time when you did that. Was there a time when you could have done that but did not? Ask God to forgive you and help you do so the next time.

Prayer

God, help me show Your fingerprint of goodness by obeying You, standing up for what is right, and caring for others' needs before my own.

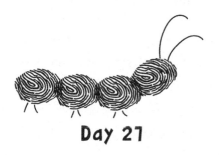

Day 27

Show Kindness

Be kind and compassionate to one another.
Ephesians 4:32

We have all experienced unkindness from others, and we all have been unkind to others at times. Jesus is the only Person in history Who showed kindness to others all the time. But God's Spirit can help us be kind. One of the fruits of the Spirit is kindness; and when Jesus comes to live in our hearts, He brings kindness with Him. We just need to allow the Holy Spirit to show kindness through our lives. Being kind means we consider others before ourselves. Instead of being selfish, we see others' needs and try to help them. We are kind not just to the people we like or those who are kind to us, but we are also kind to everyone because God is kind to everyone.

The story of the Good Samaritan is about a traveler on his way from Jerusalem to Jericho who was attacked, robbed, and left half-dead by the roadside. Two travelers, one a priest and the other a Levite, both came across the injured man but passed by on the other side. Then, a Samaritan (one of a people the Jews hated) stopped and showed compassion and kindness to the man. He took him to a safe place and paid for his care (Luke 10:30-37).

This week, ask God to show you a way to be His fingerprint of kindness to someone. Maybe you could invite someone to sit at the lunch table with you at school or include them in a game on the playground. Or you could show kindness to a neighbor by helping them carry groceries from the car to their house.

Fingerprint Fact

Early cave artists and pot makers used to "sign" their works with an impressed finger or thumbprint. Fingerprints have been discovered on ancient Babylonian seals, clay tablets, and pottery.[28] Let the fingerprint you leave behind be one of kindness.

Journal

Brainstorm and write down some ideas for showing kindness— to your family members, to your friends, and even to those whom you might not like very much.

Prayer

God, help me to be Your fingerprint of kindness to someone this week.

_____
_____
_____
_____
_____
_____
_____
_____
_____
_____
_____
_____
_____
_____
_____
_____
_____
_____
_____
_____
_____
_____
_____
_____
_____
_____

Day 28

Be Faithful

Let love and faithfulness never leave you; bind them around your neck, write them on the tablet of your heart. Then you will win favor and a good name in the sight of God and man.

Proverbs 3:3-4

Have you ever not done a chore you were supposed to do? Or have you promised someone you would do something but then decided you did not want to do it? Being faithful means you are dependable, and others can trust you to always do what you say you will do. It also means you are loyal. It means your friends can trust you to not say unkind things about them and to stand up for them. We can ask God to help us be faithful at home, at school, at church, and with our friends. He loves to give us His fruit of faithfulness, so we can show others His fingerprint in our lives.

The story of Jonathan and David in 1 Samuel 19:1-6 is a reminder of what it means to be a faithful friend. Jonathan could have been jealous of David, who was chosen by God to become king instead of him. Instead, Jonathan promised to support him and cheer him on. There may be times in your life when you are a David, chosen to be in the spotlight. In those seasons, it is a gift to have a friend like Jonathan to stand by you. There may be other times when you get to be a Jonathan to your friends, being faithful while they shine. Faithful friends support each other, and that makes God happy.

Fingerprint Fact

Your fingerprints are made up of several skin layers twisted together, kind of like a soft-serve ice cream cone.[29] Faithful friends are like those ice cream layers—woven and twisted together!

Journal

Think of a time when a friend stood by you. Write down how they showed their faithfulness. Then, think of a time when you were faithful to a friend. How did you show your faithfulness? Think of other ways you could show God's faithfulness to someone this week.

Prayer

Lord, help me to always be truthful, honest, and willing to do what I say I will do. Help me to be loyal to my friends and family and, most of all, to You.

Day 29

Be Gentle

Let your gentleness be evident to all.

Philippians 4:5

Has anyone ever said something unkind that hurt your feelings? They might not have really meant what they said, but it still hurt. It is hard to take back unkind words that have been spoken. If you have the fruit of gentleness in your life, you will stop and think before you say unkind words. In fact, gentleness means you are strong. It means you control your feelings and actions so that you do not hurt others. God's gentleness prevents us from hurting others by what we say or do.

We should always think the best of others, and that will help us react in the best way possible. Some people count to ten before they say anything when they are angry so that they will not react in the wrong way. Or you can pray, "God, help me! I want to be gentle in the way I react, but it is hard." God loves to answer those kinds of prayers.

Jesus always showed gentleness to others. People brought babies to Jesus to bless; and when His disciples tried to stop people from doing that, Jesus said, "'Let the little children come to me, and do not hinder them, for the kingdom of God belongs to such as these. Truly I tell you, anyone who will not receive the kingdom of God like a little child will never enter it'" (Luke 18:15-17). Jesus also was gentle with those who sinned and disobeyed God and with those in need. He came to show them that He is the Way.

Fingerprint Fact

About one in every six people in this country has a fingerprint record on file.[30] Just think how big God's record of fingerprints must be if every single person that has ever lived on earth has their own unique fingerprint!

Journal

Sometimes, you want to react in anger to someone who has hurt you. What are some ways you could show God's gentleness to them instead?

Prayer

Lord, help me to show gentleness in the way I react to my family and friends. I need Your help so that I can show Your fingerprint of gentleness to others.

Day 30

Practice Self-Control

**For the Spirit God gave us does not make us timid,
but gives us power, love and self-discipline.**

2 Timothy 1:7

Have you ever been tempted to do something you know is not pleasing to God—like when you really want a candy bar, and it would be so easy to just put it in your pocket without anyone seeing you steal it? It is our sinful nature that causes us to do things that displease God. Self-control is being able to control what you say and do. God gives us a conscience that helps us know right from wrong. We know deep down inside when we are about to do something that is wrong, and that is when we have to pray, "God, help me have self-control so I can do the right thing."

Self-control is also choosing to do the best thing, even when it is hard. Sometimes, we need self-control to choose the right path God has for us. We might have to give up one good thing for another. Maybe you are really good at a sport like basketball, or you play a musical instrument in the band. You will need self-control to choose to spend time practicing and developing the gifts God has given you instead of just watching TV or hanging out with your friends.

In the Bible, the apostle Paul is a good example of self-control. He says that to prepare for a race, all the runners must go into strict training if they hope to win the prize. Paul says that he, likewise, trains his body like an athlete so that he can do what God has called him to do, which is to preach the Gospel (1 Cor. 9:24-27). You will also need self-control to choose the best path God has for your life.

Fingerprint Fact

Not only do you have unique fingerprints, but you also have unique eyes, ears, and voice patterns.[31] And God gave you unique gifts and the Holy Spirit to show His love to the world.

Journal

In what areas of your life do you need self-control? Think about this past week. Maybe you did not steal anything, but you spoke unkind words to a friend. Maybe you did not have self-control when you needed to finish your homework or practice something. Write those times down in your journal and ask God to forgive you and help you in the coming week.

Prayer

Lord, thank You for always being ready to help me when I ask You to give me self-control. I want to show others Your ngerprint in my life, so I will practice self-control with Your help.

_____
_____
_____
_____
_____
_____
_____
_____
_____
_____
_____
_____
_____
_____
_____
_____
_____
_____
_____
_____
_____
_____
_____
_____

Section 4

God's Fingerprint Is Shown Through Your Gifts And Talents

Day 31

What Is Your Superpower?

There are different kinds of gifts, but the same Spirit distributes them. There are different kinds of service, but the same Lord. There are different kinds of working, but in all of them and in everyone it is the same God at work.
1 Corinthians 12:4–6

I s there a particular superhero you admire? Did you know that you do not need superpowers to be a hero? A real hero is someone who gives his or her life to something bigger than themselves. God wants you to be a hero with His power and strength and to show His love to the world.

You can begin discovering your superpower now. By learning and trying new things, you will discover the gifts and talents God has given you. Some of your gifts and talents will determine what job you have in the future. Some are natural gifts and talents, and some are spiritual gifts and talents to share with the Body of Christ. They are all important. As you grow in knowing God by reading His Word and praying, He will guide you.

In this section of the devotional, you will discover some superpowers of kids just like you, doing extraordinary things to help others. As you explore their superpowers, think about whether you might have the same superpower or a similar one. Ask God how you can use your superpower to help others right now and in the future.

Fingerprint Fact

Imagine you are a spy, and you have to get into a secret laboratory to disarm a deadly biological weapon and save the world. To get in the lab, you might have to pass several biometric scans, such as regular fingerprints, face and eye scans, and even voice fingerprints.[32]

Journal

Brainstorm (quickly write down whatever ideas come to your mind) some of the gifts you have that could help others. It might be filling a shoebox for a child in a poor country through Operation Christmas Child. It might be organizing a neighborhood collection of school supplies or clothes for those who need them. Maybe you are good at math and could help tutor a younger child in your family or at school. Maybe you love to cook and could help your mom cook a meal for a sick neighbor.

Prayer

God, thank You for giving me gifts and talents to bless others and to show Your fingerprint to a needy world. Show me some ways to use the gifts and talents You have given me now, not just when I grow up.

_____

_____

_____

_____

_____

_____

_____

_____

_____

_____

_____

_____

_____

_____

_____

_____

_____

_____

_____

_____

_____

_____

_____

_____

Day 32

Compassion

**Whoever is kind to the poor lends to the LORD,
and he will reward them for what they have done.
Proverbs 19:17**

When he was just five years old, Jankil Jackson helped his aunt distribute food at a local homeless shelter in Chicago, where he lived. When he turned eight, Jankil decided he wanted to do more to raise awareness of homelessness and help those in need, so he founded Project I Am. He began distributing what he called "Blessing Bags" to the homeless. He filled those bags with socks, deodorant, hand sanitizer, granola bars, toothbrushes, toothpaste, and bottled water. Jankil's efforts have touched over thirty thousand men, women, and children across the world.

Jesus was always kind and compassionate to people who were hurting. He healed the sick, cast out demons, and welcomed people others rejected. We, too, should have compassion on those around us who are less fortunate or hurting. Jankil felt sorrow for the suffering and misfortune of others, and he did something about it. Do you also have the superpower of compassion? How could you help others less fortunate than you?

Fingerprint Fact

Fingerprint pattern types are often genetically inherited, but the individual details that make a fingerprint unique are not.[33] We all inherit God's fingerprint of compassion, but how each of us shows it is unique to our own gifts and talents.

Journal

What do you feel compassionate about in your neighborhood or city or in the world? Write down something you might be able to do, either alone or with others, to help.

Prayer

Lord, You were always compassionate and kind to the poor and needy. Help me also to be aware of the needs of others and to help in any way I can.

_____

_____

_____

_____

_____

_____

_____

_____

_____

_____

_____

_____

_____

_____

_____

_____

_____

_____

_____

_____

_____

_____

_____

Day 33

Organization

But everything should be done in a fitting and orderly way.
I Corinthians 14:40

When Alexa Gabelle was ten years old, she created the nonprofit Bag of Books to get books into the hands of kids who might not otherwise be able to afford them. She heard about how kids often regress in their learning during the summer—especially kids from low-income families who may not have access to books. Through Bags of Books, Alexa has distributed more than 120,000 children's books to schools, homeless shelters, and children's hospitals.

It took a great deal of organization to get this nonprofit started and help it continue to grow. Do you have the superpower of organization? Do you like to organize things? Are you able to see the big picture and then break it down into small steps to accomplish what needs to be done? Organization also involves delegating tasks to other people and helping them stay organized.

God values organization. The early church had various leaders to help the church run smoothly. These included apostles (Eph. 2:20), elders (1 Peter 5:2-3), and deacons (1 Tim. 3:8-10).

Even if organization is not your superpower, you will need some organizational skills in life and your future job. You can begin to work on them right now at home and in school. Learn good ways to organize your homework and keep track of tasks at home. Your parents and teachers can help you.

Fingerprint Fact

During World War II, the FBI collected seventy million fingerprints from soldiers, foreign agents, spies, and draft dodgers. The information was organized and stored in a large warehouse nicknamed the "Fingerprint Factory."[34] It took a lot of organizational skills to carefully collect all that data and store it in the warehouse.

Journal

Write down some of your strengths in the area of organization. What are some of your weaknesses? Ask God to help you with those. If you are good with organization, list some ways you might help your younger sister or brother, a friend, or a schoolmate with their organizational skills.

Prayer

Lord, help me with my organizational skills. And if You have given me the gift of organization, help me to use it to help others.

Day 34

Perseverance

**Let us not become weary in doing good, for at the proper
time we will reap a harvest if we do not give up.**
Galatians 6:9

Nine-year-old Campbell Remess wanted to bless children at his local hospital by buying Christmas presents for them and giving them hope. His mother said no because it would cost too much money. Campbell decided that if he could not buy gifts for the children, he would make them himself.

Using his mom's sewing machine and patterns he downloaded online, he began making stuffed toys for the children. His first attempts were not great, but Campbell had perseverance. Perseverance means you keep trying in spite of difficulties and failures. You do not give up! Campbell got better and better and created many stuffed toys, bears, and blankets for the children. His idea and project grew and expanded over the years. Now a teenager, Campbell's Project 365 has touched the lives of children all over the world.

Do you remember the story of Noah in the Bible (Gen. 6:1-22)? God told Noah to build an ark, even before the rain started. God gave

Him specific instructions for how to build it and what animals Noah was to bring aboard. The Bible does not say how long it took Noah to build the Ark, but it was probably several years. Noah had to have perseverance and trust in God to complete the task God gave him.

As a Christian, you have God on your side to help you. If He has given you something to do, He will give you the strength, encouragement, and talent to do it. All you need to do is ask Him to help and guide you.

Fingerprint Fact

When fingerprinting was first done, ink and cards were used to record them. Today, digital scanners capture an image of the fingerprint. A computer then maps all the various details of the fingerprint.[35] Technology has improved a lot of things in our lives, and we can be thankful for people who persevered in inventing and discovering better ways to do things.

Journal

Do you think you have the superpower of perseverance? Are you good at not giving up on something you really want to do? In your journal, list some things that took perseverance for you to complete. Give yourself a thumbs up or a sticker. List those things that you are doing right now that need your perseverance to be done successfully. Ask God to help you.

Prayer

Lord, help me to persevere in all the things I need to do. Help me not to give up when it gets hard. Help me to remember to ask You for help and guidance.

Day 35

Hope

But those who hope in the LORD will renew their strength.
Isaiah 40:31

Ryan Hreljac has been working to make clean water accessible to people in poor areas, since he learned about the problem when he was just six years old. He began doing chores to earn money to send to organizations building wells in poor countries. When he was ten years old, he started Ryan's Well Foundation, a charity that has brought drinkable water to over eight hundred thousand people in sixteen countries. Ryan's Well Foundation also partners with schools to educate children about the problem. Ryan has brought hope to many people around the globe.

Jesus is the One Who brings real hope to people. He gives us hope while living on earth and hope for a future with Him in Heaven. He wants us to share that hope with others by telling them about Jesus. We can also demonstrate to them the hope we have in Jesus by helping meet their physical needs here on earth.

If you have hope, you believe you can do something and succeed at it. Do you have the superpower of hope? Do you have hope that others can be helped by the things you do? Sometimes, we feel very small and think that what we do will not make a difference, but everyone starts small. God can grow and expand what we do to help one or two people and enable it to help many more. We just need to trust Him and ask Him to help us.

Fingerprint Fact

To create an ink fingerprint, the person's finger is first cleaned with alcohol to remove any sweat and dried thoroughly. The person rolls his or her fingertips in ink to cover the entire fingerprint area. Then, each finger is rolled onto prepared cards from one side of the fingernail to the other. These are called rolled fingerprints.[36] While this was the first way fingerprints were done, it took a lot of time and effort. It was a small beginning for fingerprint collection and storage, but small beginnings turn into bigger and better ways of doing things.

Journal

What need do you see in your school, church, community, or world that you would like to help meet? Write down something you feel you could do to help, even if it seems very small.

Prayer

Lord, show me ways I can help meet the needs of people around me. Show me the gifts and talents You have given me to be used for this.

Day 36

Leadership

"Before I formed you in the womb, I knew you, before you were born I set you apart; I appointed you as a prophet to the nations."

Jeremiah 1:5

When Sonika Menon learned that children in Chicago often did not have the wonderful birthday parties she always had, she wanted to help. With her leadership and the help of her brother and cousins, Sonika formed the Birthday Giving Program, a nonprofit that brings birthday parties to kids and families in need. Sonika wanted these kids to feel special and to know that they mattered. Her organization partners with local shelters and organizations to provide cakes, party balloons, hats, and decorations. It also creates customized birthday bags with gifts.

When Jesus came to earth, He called twelve men to become His first disciples, or apostles. These men were not the religious leaders of the day. Most were simple, everyday people. Many of them were fishermen, and one was a hated tax collector. As Jesus taught the crowds, many other men and women followed Him and became His disciples and leaders in the Church.

If you have the gift of leadership, you know how to organize what needs to be done. Leadership also involves overseeing other workers and encouraging teamwork to get the task done. Is your superpower leadership? Do people look to you to lead them? God gives the gift of leadership to accomplish His purposes.

Our Scripture for today says that He knew Jeremiah even before he was born and called him to be a prophet. Perhaps God has called you to be a leader. But He calls you to be a servant leader—one who puts others first and does not just boss others around.

Fingerprint Fact

Since 1999, after the introduction of the Integrated AFISF system, fingerprints have been organized and stored by the FBI's Criminal Justice Services Information Division. Fingerprints, mug shots, and criminal histories can now be searched by law enforcement agencies across the country in as little as thirty minutes.[37] Organizing this integrated system was a huge feat and took lots of leadership skills by those who developed it.

Journal

Write down times you have been called upon to be a leader. Did you enjoy leading? Did you make everyone feel included? How could you be a better leader the next time? Or do you feel you are a better follower?

Prayer

Lord, thank You for the gifts You have given me. Whether I am a leader or a follower, help me be the best I can be with Your help.

Day 37

Encouragement

Therefore encourage one another and build each other up, just as in fact you are doing.

I Thessalonians 5:11

After being diagnosed with Tourette syndrome, Asperger's, and OCD, Jaylen Arnold was bullied by his peers for being different. This caused Jaylen to be anxious and feel even worse about himself. But he did not let that discourage him. He did not want others to feel what he felt, so he set out to help kids understand that each person is different and has different challenges. He founded the Jaylen Challenge Foundation, which has educated more than one hundred thousand kids on recognizing bullying behavior and understanding one another's differences.

Did you notice that inside the word "en*courage*ment," there is a smaller word—*courage*? Having courage means having the moral strength to withstand danger, fear, or difficulty. It also includes speaking out against injustice when no one else will. When you encourage someone, you are giving them courage to stand up for what is right.

Do you remember the story of David and Goliath? David was the youngest of seven brothers. While three of his older brothers had gone to war, David was still tending sheep. But when his father sent him with supplies and to check on his brothers, he saw how Goliath mocked the Israelites. Even though he was young and not a soldier, God gave him the courage to fight and conquer Goliath. David had courage because he trusted God to help him.

If you experience being bullied like Jaylen did, you know what it feels like and how it can hurt. But if you have the superpower of courage and encouragement that God supplies, you can use your experience to encourage and help others.

Fingerprint Fact

"Voice fingerprints" are not as definitive as fingerprints or DNA, but they can help distinguish one person from another.[38] God has given you a unique voice so that you can stand up for others and encourage them.

Journal

Write down a time you felt bullied by someone else. How did you react? Were you angry? Hurt? God tells us it is okay to feel these emotions, but He wants us to forgive others for hurting us. Have you asked God to help you forgive someone who hurt you? If not, pray now to forgive them. Record your prayer in your journal.

Prayer

Lord, I forgive _____ for bullying me and being mean to me. Help me not to react in the same way back to them. Instead, help me show them Your love.

_____

_____

_____

_____

_____

_____

_____

_____

_____

_____

_____

_____

_____

_____

_____

_____

_____

_____

_____

_____

_____

_____

_____

_____

Day 38

Curiosity

"For nothing will be impossible with God."
Luke 1:37 ESV

One of Sierra Leone's most famous inventors, Kelvin Doe, got started when he began looking for ways to fix local problems. His country was poor and had gone through a civil war. When he was just eleven years old, his curiosity about how things worked helped him discover how to make batteries out of acid, soda, and metal so that he could power neighborhood houses. Kelvin went on to build a community radio station out of recycled parts that he powered with a generator that was also made from reused material. Kevin later attended college and became a successful engineer.

Proverbs 25:2 says, "It is the glory of God to conceal a matter; to search out a matter is the glory of kings." In this verse, we learn that God has hidden wisdom and knowledge within His creation, and He invites us to seek it out and discover it. He has given us the curiosity and the gifts to do so, but we must make sure that our pursuits are in line with God's truth as revealed in His Word.

Do you have the superpower of curiosity? Do you like to figure out how things work and to build things? Maybe you are curious about how to help sick people by discovering new medicines. Or maybe you want to build buildings or solve problems with computers. God gives His children the gift of curiosity so they can discover more about His creation and also discover things that will help people. As you grow, you will continue to learn more and more things and discover what God wants you to do in the future.

Fingerprint Fact

Have you ever heard the statement, "Curiosity killed the cat"?

Apple created quite a buzz in 2013 when it introduced a fingerprint-coded screen lock with the iPhone 5s. Even more buzz was created when a TechCrunch writer used a cat's toe pad to create a new profile. The cat's paw worked like a fingerprint and unlocked the phone again and again when positioned correctly on the sensor.[39]

Journal

What are you curious about? What interests do you want to pursue now and in the future? Write those things in your journal. It is God Who gives you those interests and who will lead and guide you to discover how you can best serve Him and others with the talents and gifts He has given you.

Prayer

Lord, thank You for giving me curiosity and a mind that can discover new things about You and Your creation.

Day 39

Creativity

He has filled them with skill to do all kinds of work as engravers, designers, embroiderers in blue, purple and scarlet yarn and fine linen, and weavers—all of them skilled workers and designers.

Exodus 35:35

Mary Grace Henry turned her love of sewing into a way of supporting a worthwhile cause. At the age of twelve, she taught herself sewing skills and designed, created, and sold reversible headbands. She used the money she got to fund the education of one underprivileged girl. Her project then blossomed into her Reverse the Course charity, which has helped to educate many more young girls in Kenya and other underprivileged areas of the world.

Mary Grace has created dozens of different headbands, personalized bows, ponytail accessories, and special occasion hair accessories. She donates all the money from her sales to her charity, which pays for tuition and boarding costs as well as textbooks and uniforms for the girls.

Is your superpower creativity? Today's Scripture verse talks about God giving skills to those who worked on the tabernacle in the Old Testament. God has given each of us gifts and skills to do what He has called us to do. You might not create things with your hands, but perhaps you have creative thoughts about how to make something work. Creativity comes in many forms.

Fingerprint Fact

One artist created an artwork from the design of a fingerprint. He discovered there were sixty-six lines in a fingerprint. There are also sixty-six books in the Bible. The artwork has one handwritten verse from every book of the Bible, starting with "In the beginning" in Genesis 1:1 and finishing with "Hallelujah" in Revelation.[40]

Journal

Think about what you like to do and what you do well. Write down some ways you are creative in your journal.

Prayer

Thank You, God, for making me creative because You are creative. Thank You for the gifts and talents You have given me. Help me to discover what they are as I grow and to be faithful to practice those gifts and talents and to use them to bless You and others.

_____

_____

_____

_____

_____

_____

_____

_____

_____

_____

_____

_____

_____

_____

_____

_____

_____

_____

_____

_____

Day 40

Teamwork

Two are better than one, because they have a good return for their labor.

Ecclesiastes 4:9

When she was in the third grade, Katie Stagliano grew a forty-pound cabbage in her yard that helped feed 275 people at her local soup kitchen. That inspired her to create the non-profit Katie's Krops. The organization plants vegetable gardens for the sole purpose of donating food to the homeless. It allows children ages seven to sixteen who reside in the United States to apply to start a Katie's Krops garden in their community. Growers are empowered to help end hunger in their communities and towns. A young person is selected yearly to be a Katie's Krops Grower and is awarded an all-inclusive grower kit.

Katie has the superpower of teamwork, which encourages people to work together to complete a task. Teamwork means one person does not do all the work—everyone works to meet the goal. Each person on the team needs to be humble and not seek to do things their way. They need to recognize each team member's gifts and contributions.

In the Bible, we learn that the Holy Spirit gives different gifts to each member in the Body of Christ, the Church, and it takes everyone working together as a team for the Church to be what God wants it to be (1 Cor. 12:27-30).

Fingerprint Fact

It takes a lot of teamwork to collect, analyze, and store fingerprints and other data we use for identification today, including that of law enforcement officers, fingerprints analysts, data processing specialists, biologists, and chemists.

Journal

Have you ever been part of a team that worked on a project together? How did it feel to be part of a team? Was it hard or easy? How can you encourage teamwork on a task or project you might be a part of at home, school, or church?

Prayer

Lord, whenever I am on a team, help me to be a good example of what it means to be a team member. Help me be humble and contribute my part so that the task can be completed well.

Congratulations!

You have successfully completed all forty *Fingerprint Devotions*. I trust you have learned how special you are to God and how He uniquely created you for a purpose. Be sure to check out all the fun resources in the back of this book to learn more about fingerprints and to find lots of art projects you can do using your fingerprints.

Endnotes

1   *Merriam-Webster, s.v.* "unique," accessed July 30, 2023, https://www.merriam-webster.com/dictionary/unique.

2   "A Simplified Guide to Fingerprint Analysis: Principles," Forensic Science Simplified, Global Forensic and Justice Center, last modified 2013, https://www.forensicsciencesimplified.org/prints/principles.html.

3   "The Fingerprints of God Are All around Us. Just Take a Look!," Great Life Publishing, last modified March 19, 2021, https://faithhub.net/fibonacci-fingerprint.

4   T. Trimpe, "Fingerprints," Northeast Georgia Council, BSA, accessed September 5, 2021, https://www.nega-bsa.org/files/28164/Forensic-Fingerprinting--Training-Slides.

5   Donald B. DeYoung, "Is Every Star Different?," in *Astronomy and the Bible: Questions and Answers*, 2nd ed. (Grand Rapids, MI: Baker Books, 2000), https://christiananswers.net/q-eden/star-differences.html.

6   "A Simplified Guide to Fingerprint Analysis: Principles," ibid.

7   Melissa Healy, "Move Over DNA. Scientists Can Identify You Based on the Unique Pattern of Proteins in Your Hair," Los Angeles Times online, September 9, 2016, https://www.latimes.com/science/sciencenow/la-sci-sn-hair-protein-identification-20160907-snap-story.html.

8   "A Simplified Guide to Fingerprint Analysis: Principles," ibid.

9   "Ten Facts about Fingerprints," Tensor Plc, accessed June 2, 2020, https://www.tensor.co.uk/blog/news/10-facts-about-fingerprints.

10   *Merriam-Webster, s.v.* "dermatoglyphics," accessed August 2, 2022, https://www.merriamwebster.com/dictionary/dermatoglyphic.

11   "What's So Special about This Painting That Its Price Is $830 Million?," Science ABC, last modified January 22, 2022, https://www.scienceabc.com/soci-science/why-is-mona-lisa-so-famous-worth-cost-today-meaning.html (page no longer available as of June 24, 2023).

12   "A Simplified Guide to Fingerprint Analysis: Principles," ibid.

13   Ada McVean, "Koalas Have Fingerprints Just Like Humans," Office for Science and Society, McGill University, accessed September 5, 2020, https://www.mcgill.ca/oss/article/did-you-know/koalas-have-fingerprints-just-humans.

14 Stephanie Watson, "How Fingerprinting Works," HowStuffWorks, last modified March 24, 2008, https://science.howstuffworks.com/fingerprinting5.htm.

15   Trimpe, "Fingerprints."

16   "A Simplified Guide to Fingerprint Analysis: How It's Done," Global Forensic and Justice Center, accessed July 3, 2021, https://www.forensicsciencesimplified.org/prints/how.html.

17 Anne Marie Helmenstine, "No Two Snowflakes Alike—True or False," ThoughtCo, Dotdash Media Inc., last modified March 2, 2020, https://www.thoughtco.com/why-all-snowflakes-are-different-609167.

18   Dory Gascueña, "Science in Your Hands: What Your Fingerprints Say about You," OpenMind BBVA, June 6, 2017, https://www.bbvaopenmind.com/en/science/research/science-in-your-hands-what-your-fingerprints-say-about-you.

19   "9 Facts You Didn't Know About Dogs That Will Leave You Pawsitively Amazed," The Holidog Times EN, last modified February 24, 2016, https://www.holidogtimes.com/9-facts-you-didnt-know-about-dogs-that-will-leave-you-pawsitively-amazed/ (page no longer available as of June 24, 2023).

20   Gascueña, ibid.

21   Ibid.

22   Chris Higgins, "Watch Ultra-Closeup Video of Sweat Glands on Fingertips," Mental Floss, March 19, 2017, video, 1:13, https://www.mentalfloss.com/article/93389/watch-ultra-closeup-video-sweat-glands-fingertips.

23 "Ten Facts about Fingerprints," ibid.

24 DentistryIQ Editors, "New Oral Features Can Be Considered Unique as a Fingerprint," Dentistry IQ, Endeavor Business Media Dental Group, January 27, 2014, https://www.dentistryiq. com/dentistry/article/16359712/new-oral-features-can-be-considered-unique-as-a-fingerprint.com.

25 Watson, ibid.

26 Ibid.

27 "Fascinating Ancient History of Fingerprints," MessageToEagle. com, March 4, 2016, https://www.messagetoeagle.com/fascinating-ancient-history-of-fingerprints.

28 Ibid.

29 Kate Horowitz, "15 Unique Facts about Fingerprints," Mental Floss, April 15, 2016, https://www.mentalfloss.com/ article/78169/15-unique-facts-about-fingerprints.

30 Watson, ibid.

31 Ibid.

32 Ibid.

33 Glenn Langenburg, "Are One's Fingerprints Similar to Those of His or Her Parents in Any Discernable Way?," Scientific American, January 24, 2005, https://www.scientificamerican. com/article/are-ones-fingerprints-sim.

34 Horowitz, ibid.

35 Watson, ibid.

36 Ibid.

37 Ibid.

38 Ibid.

39 Horowitz, ibid.

40 "The Story of 'God's Fingerprint,'" God's fingerprints, February 7, 2017, https://godsfingerprints.co/blogs/blog/the-story-of-gods-fingerprint.

Bibliography

DentistryIQ Editors. "New Oral Features Can Be Considered Unique as a Fingerprint." Dentistry IQ. January 27, 2014. https://www.dentistryiq.com/dentistry/article/16359712/new-oral-features-can-be-considered-unique-as-a-fingerprint.com.

DeYoung, Donald B. "Is Every Star Different?" In *Astronomy and the Bible: Questions and Answers*. 2nd ed. Grand Rapids, MI: Baker Books, 2000. https://christiananswers.net/q-eden/star-differences.html.

"Fascinating Ancient History of Fingerprints." MessageToEagle.com. March 4, 2016. https://www.messagetoeagle.com/fascinating-ancient-history-of-fingerprints.

"Fingerprints of God Are All around Us, The. Just Take a Look!" Great Life Publishing, last modified March 19, 2021. https://faithhub.net/fibonacci-fingerprint.

"Five young people creating a better world." CNN online. December 11, 2018. https://www.cnn.com/2018/12/05/world/cnnheroes-young-wonders-2018/index.html.

"From coding to literacy: These youth are changing the game." CNN online. December 16, 2017. https://edition.cnn.com/2017/12/13/us/cnn-heroes-2017-young-wonders/index.html.

Gascueña, Dory. "Science in Your Hands: What Your Fingerprints Say About You." OpenMind BBVA, June 6, 2017. https://www.bbvaopenmind.com/en/science/research/science-in-your-hands-what-your-fingerprints-say-about-you.

Healy, Melissa. "Move over DNA. Scientists Can identify You Based on the Unique Pattern of Proteins in Your Hair." Los Angeles Times online. September 9, 2016. https://www.latimes.com/

science/sciencenow/la-sci-sn-hair-protein-identification-20160907-snap-story.html.

Helmenstine, Anne Marie. "No Two Snowflakes Alike—True or False." ThoughtCo. Dotdash Media Inc., last modified March 2, 2020. https://www.thoughtco.com/why-all-snowflakes-are-different-609167.

Higgins, Chris. "Watch Ultra-Closeup Video of Sweat Glands on Fingertips." Mental Floss. March 19, 2017. https://www.mentalfloss.com/article/93389/watch-ultra-closeup-video-sweat-glands-fingertips.

Horowitz, Kate. "15 Unique Facts about Fingerprints." Mental Floss. April 15, 2016. https://www.mentalfloss.com/article/78169/15-unique-facts-about-fingerprints.

Langenburg, Glenn. "Are One's Fingerprints Similar to Those of His or Her Parents in Any Discernable Way?" *Scientific American.* January 24, 2005. https://www.scientificamerican.com/article/are-ones-fingerprints-sim.

McVean, Ada. "Koalas Have Fingerprints Just Like Humans." Office for Science and Society. McGill University, accessed September 5, 2020. https://www.mcgill.ca/oss/article/did-you-know/koalas-have-fingerprints-just-humans.

Merriam-Webster. S.v. "unique." Accessed July 30, 2023. https://www.merriam-webster.com/dictionary/unique.

Merriam-Webster. S.v. "dermatoglyphics." Accessed August 2, 2022. https://www.merriamwebster.com/dictionary/dermatoglyphic.

"9 Facts You Didn't Know About Dogs That Will Leave You Pawsitively Amazed." Holidog Times EN. Last modified February 24, 2016. https://www.holidogtimes.com/9-facts-you-didn't-know-about-dogs-that-will-leave-you-pawsitively-amazed.

Savedge, Jenn. "Meet 20 Kids Who Are Changing the World Right Now." Treehugger.com. May 28, 2020. https://www.treehugger.com/meet-kids-who-are-changing-world-4868568.

Schubak, Adam. "Read the Stories of 40 Incredible Kids Who Have Changed the World." Good Housekeeping online.

October 8, 2020. https://www.goodhousekeeping.com/life/inspirational-stories/g5188/kids-who-changed-the-world.

"Simplified Guide to Fingerprint Analysis, A: How It's Done." Global Forensic and Justice Center, accessed July 3, 2021. https://www.forensicsciencesimplified.org/prints/how.html.

"Simplified Guide to Fingerprint Analysis, A: Principles." Global Forensic and Justice Center, last modified 2013. https://www.forensicsciencesimplified.org/prints/principles.html.

"Story of 'God's Fingerprint,' The." God's fingerprints. February 7, 2017. https://godsfingerprints.co/blogs/blog/the-story-of-gods-fingerprint.

"Ten Facts about Fingerprints." Tensor Plc. Accessed June 2, 2020. https://www.tensor.co.uk/blog/news/10-facts-about-fingerprints.

Trimpe, T. "Fingerprints." Northeast Georgia Council, BSA. Accessed September 5, 2021. https://www.nega-bsa.org/files/28164/Forensic-Fingerprinting---Training-Slides.

Watson, Stephanie. "How Fingerprinting Works." HowStuffWorks. Last modified March 24, 2008. https://science.howstuffworks.com/fingerprinting5.htm.

"What's So Special About This Painting That Its Price Is $830 Million?" Science ABC. Last modified January 22, 2022. https://www.scienceabc.com/soci-science/why-is-mona-lisa-so-famous-worth-cost-today-meaning.html.

Recommended Resources

Books
Cox, Kris and Kris Hage. *Growing the Fruit of the Spirit: A Bible-based Unit Study*. Independently Published, 2022.

Rivera, Jennifer. *The Work of Your Hand: Fingerprints, God & You!* Green Forest: Master Books, 2019.

Emberley, Ed. *Ed Emberley's Fingerprint Drawing Book*. Boston: LB Kids, 2005.

Videos
Carpenter, Michael E. "How to Explain Fingerprints to Children." Leaf Group. https://classroom.synonym.com/explain-fingerprints-children-8787591.html.

"Forensic Science Behind God's Fingerprint Design, The." Answers in Genesis. August 1, 2019. YouTube video, 55:43. https://www.youtube.com/watch?v=PulVntyieU4.

Products
2 X Lee Inkless Fingerprint Pad (S03027)
https://www.amazon.com/gp/product/B0128964NM/
ref=ox_sc_act_title_1?smid=A31EVTLIC13ORD&th=1.

Fingerprint Art Set for Kids
https://www.amazon.com/dp/B07QGPYLX8/
ref=cm_sw_em_r_mt_dp_CKAD55oDDXQBMBMWTJNC.

About the Author

With a personal goal to "Pray Often! Inspire Others! Create Beauty!" Sandra pens articles, blogs, and books to encourage Christians in their personal walk with God. She has a passion to help kids understand how uniquely created and loved by God they are and to help them discover their God-given purpose in life. Sandra is also a prayer warrior, prayer encourager, and the author of an award-winning small group/personal study on prayer, *Lord, It's Boring in My Prayer Closet: How to Revitalize Your Prayer Life*.

Sandra has been a teacher and writer for most of her professional life. She taught English, journalism, and special education in both public and private schools. As a journalist and writer, Sandra has published hundreds of news, profiles, travel, and lifestyle stories for various publications. She also writes nonfiction and children's picture books.

Sandra lives in coastal North Carolina and enjoys spending time with her husband, their daughter, son-in-law, and their French bulldog puppy. A photography buff, she has been known to wander off and get lost while taking photos. When not writing, Sandra enjoys traveling, walking on ocean piers and the beach, eating local seafood, and curling up with a good mystery or historical fiction book.

For more information about
Sandra Kay Chambers
and
Fingerprint Devotions
please visit:

www.sandrakaychambers.com

www.instagram.com/SandraKayChambers

www.facebook.com/SandraKayChambersAuthor

www.pinterest.com/sandrakaychamberswriter

5-Minute Parenting: www.sandrakaychambers.com/podcast

Downloadable Free Activity Book with Coloring Pages, Activity Sheets, and Fingerprint Fact Cards available for download at Sandra's website.

Ambassador International's mission is to magnify the Lord Jesus Christ and promote His Gospel through the written word.

We believe through the publication of Christian literature, Jesus Christ and His Word will be exalted, believers will be strengthened in their walk with Him, and the lost will be directed to Jesus Christ as the only way of salvation.

For more information about
AMBASSADOR INTERNATIONAL
please visit:

www.ambassador-international.com

To help further our mission, please consider leaving us—or ask your parents to leave us—a review on social media, your favorite retailer's website, Goodreads or Bookbub, or our website, and be sure to check out some of our other books!

More for Kids from Ambassador International

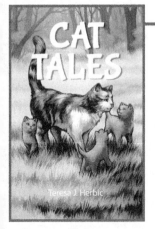

Cat Tales is a practical and fun way to teach children about the significant fruit of the Spirit, while enjoying the sensational adventures of nine real cats. These cats tell stories from their own perspective as they learn about the importance of God's plan, and each exhibit a fruit of the Spirit.

Also available is *Dog Tales*.

Many children today are struggling with depression and anxiety. In *More Than a Conqueror: A Christian Kid's Guide to Winning the War Against Worry*, licensed clinical social worker Laura Kuehn provides a way for children and parents to work together to face their Worry Weasels. With practical tips and engaging activities, this book will provide any child with what they need to overcome their anxieties and live their lives able to face whatever may come their way.

Marcy Lytle wrote these devotions for her own children, to make the Bible real and practical in their lives. This fun devotional includes many illustrations with hands on projects that your children will love, and you will love the time that your family will spend together learning about God.

Made in United States
Orlando, FL
11 November 2023